Thought this book would come in useful as it combines two of your favourite things....

xxx

First published 2007
© Mark Pallis 2007

Published by Wooden Books Ltd.
8A Market Place, Glastonbury, Somerset

British Library Cataloguing in Publication Data
Pallis, M.
Lipsmacking Backpacking

A CIP catalogue record for this book is
available from the British Library

ISBN 1 904263 41 0

Printed and bound in England by
The Cromwell Press, Trowbridge, Wiltshire.
100% recycled papers supplied by Paperback.

LIPSMACKING BACKPACKING

HOW TO COOK ON YOUR TRAVELS

by

Mark Pallis

with illustrations by Fleur Sandalls

This book is dedicated to Mum and Dad, to whom I owe my love of cooking and of writing. Special thanks to Laurent, Rob, and especially to Benedetta.

Spaghetti cooked in snow, with raisins:
Eating out in style on Mount Kenya.

Check out: www.lipsmackingbackpacking.com,
www.spw.org, www.gapyear.com

Contents

INTRODUCTION

Backpacking is all about adventure and new experiences: doing things you wouldn't normally do, trying things you wouldn't normally try, and taking chances. On my first trip, I wasn't quite so daring when it came to food. I was surrounded by delicious, fresh local produce, but I ate mainly from a tin.

Why would anyone, myself included, choose to scrape overcooked baked beans from the bottom of a pan instead of rustling up something fresh? My epiphany came on Tiwi Beach in Kenya. I was smearing peanut butter on a piece of bread, as I did every lunchtime, when a local fish-seller came by, pushing his bicycle through the sand. In his bike-basket, peeping out from under big green banana leaves, were fresh prawns, caught that morning. I remember looking at them wistfully, trying my hardest, but failing, to remember a recipe. Someone bought a bagful. I went over to the him and asked, 'what are you going to do with them?' 'Eat them of course' he replied, looking at me like I was a bit deranged. 'But what recipe are you going to use?' I said. Then he told me something that would change the way I cooked forever: "There is no recipe, I'm just going to cook it."

I should add at this point that the guy in question was French, so this came out as "Zere is no resipee, ahm juss going t'couk eet." I don't want to get melodramatic, but it was a big moment for me. He'd uttered what I took to be a sacred truth – and the French accent made it even more hallowed. No recipe? My world was crashing down. What about scales and measuring jugs? How are you supposed to know when things are ready?

I put these questions to the back of my mind, put my peanut butter sandwich down, and watched as he washed the prawns, put them on the fire and, in no time at all, right in front of my eyes, these intimidating, grey little crustaceans had turned into juicy, tender pink delicacies. Having spent the past 20 minutes watching in rapt attention, I found myself invited to lunch, and what a lunch it was: the best meal of my travels up to that point!

When I got back to the village where I was living, I was determined to put this new philosophy into practice. I mucked around a bit. I had a few stonking successes (like curried browned matoke with fried chicken) and an equal number of hideous disasters (boiled cabbage soup … don't remind me), but mainly everything worked out pretty well. I felt liberated by the idea that I was in control of what I was cooking, and I had loads of fun.

The idea for this book came as I was scanning the shelves in my local bookstore, trying to find a cookbook to take out on my next trip so that I could broaden my culinary horizons. But nothing was right. It was all just recipes recipes recipes. I don't have anything against that in itself: if you're at home, with supermarkets all around, it's easy to check a cookbook, decide what to cook and then go and find all the ingredients. But when you're backpacking, it doesn't work like that. Trying to follow a recipe off the beaten track is like trying to tell a story backwards. We can't decide what recipe to follow first because probably some, most or all of the ingredients won't be available. The backpacker's story begins with the ingredients: we see what's on offer, see how to cook it, put it all together and voila, there is our meal.

So this book is designed to help you deal with whatever a market might throw at you. I hope that you find it helpful and fun.

Just a quick concluding word on safety for you and for the environment. Cooking on an open fire is a lot of fun, but it can have grave consequences if it starts a bush-fire. Take all proper precautions. Also, be thoughtful when you're collecting firewood. Deforestation is a major issue all over the world, so always get wood from a sustainable source.

Of course, always make sure that the food is safe to eat, and take care of yourself and your surroundings when cooking on an open fire. So, pack your rucksack, get excited, go off the beaten track, take chances, and cook!

Equipment

Basically, all you need is an excellent knife, a pot or two and something to cook on. The pot is central to cooking. You can use it for everything – even to eat from. There are two main options: buy it out there or bring it out with you. You will find that they will be cheaper abroad, although in some countries only light moulded aluminium pans tend to be readily available.

There is a direct relation between the weight of a pan and how good it is (damn!). A light pan will bend and buckle from heat and general wear and tear. Once that flatness has gone, the heat will no longer be uniformly distributed and food will burn in places when you fry, and things will start sticking to the bottom more easily. Best advice is to see what's available in your local supermarket and camping shop: the longer you're staying for, and the more you're going to be roughing it, the heavier the pots should be.

The pot should have a lid, but if you want to keep weight to a minimum, use a metal plate. As well as being a useful plate, these also make great 'wafters', fans that you can use for turning fledgling fires into raging infernos. Some pots have nifty handles, which are useful for attaching the pot to your bag and during cooking. As far as the second, 'sauce etc.', pot is concerned, save space by buying one that fits inside the first.

A Swiss Army knife, Leatherman or other good quality pocket-knife is essential. Experience taught me that scrimping on this is a false economy. You don't need to buy something with a whole armoury built in, a sharp knife or two, a bottle or can opener and maybe some scissors is sufficient. A big knife can also be good for things like chopping up fresh coconuts or hacking wood, but unless you want to spend ages in the airport security room and customs, buy that when you're out there.

As far as other things are concerned, it's really up to you and how light you want to travel. A general kit list might include: a fork and spoon; a big metal cup; a metal plate (but if your pot has a lid bring a plastic plate or bowl as they're lighter); pan scourers for cleaning; stock cubes or dry garlic powder..

For barbecue cooking, you'll need a metal grate, or chicken wire. Invariably, these things just tend to be lying around, especially at beaches, all over the world. If, amazingly, there is nothing or you're making kebabs you will need skewers. You can make your own from a branch, but take care that the tree is not poisonous, that you're not damaging the tree, disturbing wildlife or the tree's owner. Take off any side shoots and remove the bark. Using your knife, make a point at one end and you have a skewer. Soak it in water for an hour or so before you use it to prevent it burning.

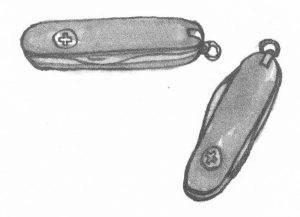

What To Cook On:

What we cook on makes a big difference to our experience: gas stoves are quick and efficient, great when you're in a crowded campsite or in a hurry, but the small ring of blue flames doesn't really rev us up for a "cum by ya". Barbecues and wood stoves are for when you've moved down a gear, and are taking it easy. Two golden rules: safety and hygiene. Never start a fire if it is prohibited, if there is not sufficient open space, or if there is anything that could be a fire hazard nearby. Clear a large area around the heat source before lighting it. Always be sure that you know what you are doing, always supervise children. Always have sufficient water or sand handy to put out the fire. For hygiene, do not cook close to toilets or drains. All in all just use your common sense, but if in doubt, do not take a risk.

Portable Stove

The three most common fuel types are gas, meths and paraffin (these are sometimes known by other names in other countries). Each stove, be it a trangia or mini-gaz stove will vary, so you should follow the specific instructions for your product. The basic point is to make sure that all parts are correctly fitted and tightly screwed, that there is adequate fuel and that the stove is on flat ground. Make sure that it is sheltered if it is windy, and that you keep your fuel bottle well away from the flames.

Charcoal Stove

Far less portable (they weigh a ton) but readily available in Africa and other parts of the world is the charcoal stove. Put some charcoal into the main body, filling it so as to be level with the top rim – don't exceed this otherwise your pot will be sitting on the coals and not on the stove. To light it, put some ash onto a piece of paper and pour some meths or paraffin onto the ash. Light and place it under the coals via the little door. I've included some tear-out pages at the end of the book that you can use as emergency firelighters. Leave it for

a while and fan the coals until they have caught fire. You might need to fan pretty vigorously. When the coals have caught and are starting to turn grey at the edges, put on your pot.

BARBECUE (CHARCOAL OR WOOD)

Obtain some dry wood or charcoal and keep it in a pile away from where you want to cook. It's always good to get more than you think you'll need. Deforestation is a major issue in many countries, plus wood, even dead wood, is often a vital habitat for a range of forest species. Ensure that the wood you're going to burn is coming from a sustainable source.

The secret of a good burn is adequate ventilation and dry wood, but the secret of good cooking is to have a stable base. Arrange three or four similarly sized, flattish stones into a triangle and make sure that your pot can balance securely on top. Make a small pyramid of kindling and easy to burn things like dry bark and light it. Put more sticks on as the fire catches and then put on your pot. Feed the new sticks or charcoal in from the sides as they are needed – it's best to get some quite long, thick, dry pieces and you can just push the end inwards as they burn. If you have a grate, pop that on the stones and there's your barbecue – but don't forget to wait until the flames have died down before putting the food on.

How to Cook (a quick guide!)

Wherever you go, whoever you are, whatever you eat, there are really only five ways of cooking: cooking with water, frying, pressure cooking, oven cooking, and using radiant heat (barbecuing and grilling).

As a backpacker, unless you're training for some weightlifting championships, you're not going to carry a pressure cooker and that oven is going nowhere. *Lipsmacking Backpacking* is about cooking with water, barbecuing and frying.

Cooking with water simply means steaming or putting ingredients into heated water (maybe containing salt or other aromatic ingredients). When you boil something to excess it goes soggy and mushy because it has absorbed too much water. You need to get the right amount of water into your ingredient, and it's not difficult if you know the secret: the time to cook properly varies according to an ingredient's size, tenderness and texture as well as the weather, the ferocity of your heat-source and the thickness of your pan. In short, it always depends. The best way to know when something is done is to follow the rough cooking-time estimates I provide, then stick a knife in to see how soft it is, or taste a bit.

As some of the cooking water is absorbed by what you put in the pot, if the water has a flavour, the ingredients take on that flavour: we all know that cooking pasta in salted water gives you salted pasta. Make the most of whatever herbs, spices or flavourings are available. Really, your imagination is the limit. Think of a taste or aroma you like, add some to your pot, boil up your food and hey presto, the food now has a hint of that flavour.

Barbecuing is my second backpacking technique. The heat from the charcoal or wood penetrates the food directly and cooks it. The only thing that can go wrong is that you can over or undercook your food. You can't control the temperature of the fire itself, but you can control how close you put the ingredient to the heat. The closer it is, the hotter it gets. The point is to get the heat to penetrate the ingredient evenly and thoroughly. For small things like kebabs this means you need to move them around, but for larger, thicker foods, like meat or fish steaks, you just need to turn them over a few times. Always check that meat and fish are cooked all the way through – unless you want it rare and you're sure of the quality of the meat.

Just as the water will flavour the things you boil, so the smoke from what you burn will flavour what you barbecue. Add anything you fancy to your fire: herbs, spices, leaves from fruit trees – whatever is to hand (apart from old tyres or plastic bags!).

Frying involves putting oil, butter, lard or fat from meat into a hot pot, or onto your ingredient, and then putting the ingredient in the pot. Because the heat is so great, and the oil is transmitting it to the ingredient, frying cooks things quickly: whether a vegetable or fish dusted with flour, a pattie or steak. Often frying is just the start of the cooking process. You might fry onions, garlic, spices and meat then add water and softer vegetables to make a stew.

Oil can be a bit of a nuisance to carry around with you as it manages to find its way into clothes and towels etc. Even marge in a tub will get slippy if the weather's hot. It's best to wrap them in a plastic bag and then wrap that in an old T-shirt or something and keep them, if you can, in a separate part of your backpack.

9

BREAK IT DOWN

So, we've got our kit, we've got our techniques – let's get cooking. But where to start? There's an almost infinite number of ingredients out there and what if you can't get a particular kind of food in the place you are travelling to? I take solace in the words of those wise rappers who say "Break it down!"

Just as there's only a few cooking methods, there's really only a few basic types of food. When I backpack I think in terms of four food types: staples; meat & fish; vegetables and fruits.

"Staples" is a catch-all term to describe all starchy foods. Heavy and full of carbohydrate, they really fill you up and give you energy. Staples include everything in the 'root' family (potatoes, sweet potatoes, cassava, yams, turnips, swede etc.); bananas; all pulses; all rice; wheat and corn based food such as Polenta, Ugali/Posho; cous cous. A staple will probably be present in every meal you make, either on the side or mixed in with other ingredients.

By meat and fish I mean beef, pork, lamb, chicken, etc., plus all fish and shellfish. I think we all know what vegetables and fruits are.

What no-one ever told me was that you can use the same techniques to cook almost all similar types of food. What works for a potato will also work for yams, plantain or turnips. Ditto for lamb or beef, cod or Nile perch and ditto for onions, leek or fennel.

The rest of this book is arranged into sections. Follow the techniques and apply them to whatever you find in your local market wherever you happen to be in the world.

Nothing stands between you and a feast. Your imagination and your preference are the limits. Just have a go!

STAPLES

MEATS & FISH

VEGETABLES

FRUIT

"THERE ARE
BASICALLY
FOUR TYPES
OF FOOD"

Roots

As for all staples, the main way of cooking roots is in water, normally lightly salted – but do try adding a pinch of sugar, if often helps bring out the flavour. Cooking times, for all of the talk you might have heard about precise measurements, will always vary. Size, texture, quantity, the type of staple you're cooking, whether you're an 'al dente' person – all these affect the cooking time. All you're really doing is letting the water penetrate the staple: the longer you leave it, the more water gets absorbed. The basic point is to have a go: have a look around the market, see what's there, talk to people, buy something, clean it, cook it, taste it to see if it is ready and just eat it.

You can always identify roots in the market as they tend to be hard and muddy. All have different flavours, lots of carbohydrate and low fat – forget faddish diets, these are perfect for a hi-energy backpacker.

The way to prepare them is to peel or scrub them, cutting out any bad bits or eyes. Beware of green or soft parts – cut them out, or best of all, discard the entire root. Just under the skin is where most of the nutrients are so peel them as closely as you can. Rinse them then place them in cold water, bring it to the boil and keep them boiling for about twenty minutes. If they aren't done after that, just pop them back on the heat for a while: it's always better to undercook something and then heat it a bit longer than overcook it and eat a soggy mess.

One school of thought says that you don't need to do anything to roots when serving them save for giving them a quick sprinkling of salt. That is true – it's worked well for the British for centuries! Roots absorb some of the water you cook them in so you can add flavour to them by flavouring the water. Try adding bay leaves, lemongrass, or a smashed fennel root to your water. The other alternative is to flavour root directly by sprinkling some herbs or spices on it after it is cooked. The key thing is to use your imagination. Serve them boiled or mashed, to the side of plate, or use the mash as a base onto which to put your other ingredients. Try chopping the boiled root into pieces about a couple of centimetres thick, putting one piece in the middle of your plate, stacking a couple of slices of vegetables on top, and then stacking another smaller slice of root on the top. If you've made a sauce, pour this around the side of the plate – that's all there is to the artistic heaps that you see the TV chefs creating!

IMPORTANT: some roots contain amydalen, a cyanide compound, and need to be specially prepared first if you don't want Ms Marple snooping around. Always ask, never take a risk.

SLIGHTLY LESS IMPORTANT: If you go to a market in Australia, don't ask them for a root, as it means something slightly different over there.

BOILED ROOTS:

Root, Water, Salt and pepper

Prepare the root. If the roots are large, cut them in half or quarters – say the size of an egg. The smaller the chunk the quicker it cooks. Rinse them. Drop them in a pot of salted water and bring it to the boil – making sure that the roots are always totally submerged. Boil them for about twenty minutes. The time basically depends on how big the pieces are, so the best thing is to taste them or prod them with your fork and when you can break them, they're done. Drain, serve and season with salt and pepper. If you've only got one heat source, boil them for about 15 minutes, then take them off the heat and put a lid on the pot. They'll keep cooking in the water whilst you make the rest of your meal, and then you can pop them back on the heat at the end for a quick blast.

JACKET ROOT:

Root

The simplest way of cooking a root on the barbecue is to pierce it once deeply, wrap it in foil or banana leaves, and put in on your grate. Leave it for about an hour to an hour and a half, turning every 15 minutes. When it is done, it will be soft enough for a knife to be stuck in with no resistance. Scoop out the middle and eat it. If you're in a bit of a rush you can make a deep, clean incision from the top to bottom and that will speed up to cooking time a little, although it will make the root dryer inside.

If you're wondering what to do with the skins of your jacket potato, try barbecuing them. Make sure that there is a thin layer of flesh attached to the skin, dribble some oil over the top and put them on your grate for 4 – 5 minutes until they are crispy.

SHALLOW FRIED ROOTS:

Root, Water, Butter/Margarine/Oil/Lard/Fat, Onions/garlic, Salt & Pepper

Prepare the root and cut into wedges and cook in water for five minutes less than normal. Transfer them to a pan with quite a lot of hot oil, into which you have already had some chopped onions and or peeled and smashed garlic on the go for about 5 minutes. Make sure that the bottom of the wedges are sitting in oil. They will bubble away. Turn them over, taking care not to break them. After about 15 minutes they should be golden. Season with salt and pepper. The thinner you cut them the quicker they will cook, but of course, the more likely they are to break apart. You don't have to have the onions/garlic, but they add flavour – just as does adding some spice to the oil.

If you cut the root very thin, you can fry them without boiling them first – like crisps. This will take 15 to 20 minutes. Do make sure that you have dried the root carefully beforehand.

14

Mashed Roots:

Root, Water, Butter/Margarine/Oil/Milk, Salt & Pepper

Want decent mash or a slop? I go for the former, so make sure that the root is as dry as possible and this means that you should not chop them up if you can help it – the smaller the pieces, the soggier the end results. Follow the steps as for simple mash and when the root is done, drain the water from the pot and smash them with a spoon, fork or whatever. If you have butter, oil, or milk you can add it, to make a smoother, creamier mash. Season with salt and pepper. Mash is best enjoyed straight, but you can also use it a base and add whatever else you like: cooked vegetables; herbs or spices. Nutmeg; raw chillies; mustard are my favourites, but, as always, you can try whatever's to hand.

To make a mash-pattie, wait for the mash to cool down a bit, dust your hands in flour and grab a handful of mash. Relive your childhood and savour the feeling of it squidging through your fingers. Shape it into a flattish ball that fits in the palm of your hand. When you've done as many as you want, pop them in your pot with some sizzling oil on the bottom and cook them for a few minutes each side. Take care when you turn them over or they'll disintegrate. If eggs are available, add a beaten egg to your potato mix to make it stick together better. These egg-patties can also be cooked on the barbecue. You can add whatever you want to your pattie: nuts, cooked vegetables, spices, herbs, even a little bit of fruit, like raisins, if you're feeling adventurous.

BANANAS

Although they may look simply like unripe bananas, green bananas, plantain or matoke, as they are variously known, are floury, very filling and when cooked have a wonderful aroma. There are a number of different varieties which vary from country to country and region to region. They are well worth trying. The principle for cooking is the usual one: water and heat must be absorbed. You should allow two or three bananas per person, depending on their size (that's the size of the banana and the size of the person).

There are not many hints to serving banana, it is all pretty simple: serve it to the side either boiled, mashed or fried, or as a base onto which your pour your sauce, or on a kebab. For a special occasion you could cook the banana whole and then serve up two of them side by side on a washed banana leaf. Next you can arrange some salad between the two bananas and then place a piece of meat (or some nuts) on the top. Finish it off by placing a segment of citrus fruit on the top.

The other hint is on what to do with the black, gummy residue that you always get on your hands when you peel them. You can reduce it by carefully washing the banana with its skin still on. Next, change the water and peel the banana while it is still submerged. Rinse your knife often. A short cut to getting the residue off your hands is to dab the affected spots with paraffin. Of course, you've got to make sure that you clean your hands again before cooking anything else!

Boiled Banana:

Banana, Water, Salt & pepper

Wash the outside of the banana, cut off the ends and cut into two pieces at the middle. Run a slit along one side and put in a pot of boiling water for about 20 minutes. Slip the skin off, season with salt and pepper and serve.

They can, once bananas are cooked, also be smashed to make a nice mash. This mash can either be eaten straight or fried, either on its own, or with some onions or garlic for about five minutes to give it a nice gentle browning and a deeper flavour. If you were at home you might also add some balsamic vinegar and parmesan – ah, the sweet dreams of the hungry backpacker!

Banana chips:

Banana, Oil/Fat/Butter/Margarine, Spices (optional)

Peel the banana with a sharp knife and chop it into thin slices – about the width of a 2 euro coin, or narrower. Put them in a pot with hot oil and shallow fry for about seven minutes or until golden. You can add spices to the oil if you've got any and are up for it.

Jacket Banana:

Banana, Salt & pepper

Put the banana on your grate, or in the fire itself for about 40 minutes or until the outside is totally black and you can feel that the middle is soft. Carefully take it out, cut it open and scoop out the middle. Season with salt and pepper.

GRAINS - RICE

Big, small, or powdered, grains are a backpacker's friend. Even the biggest kind of grain, rice, is still very space-efficient and rucksack friendly. You can fit grains into small corners and nearly-full pockets. As far as the taste is concerned, it's pretty much up to you. Try a plate of plain, fluffy, stickyish white rice for breakfast or cook sweet fruity polenta as an accompaniment to fried chicken, or make face-slapping tangy cous cous to serve with a fresh salad. Don't forget that grains absorb much more of the water which they are cooked in than roots or bananas, so giving the water flavour will give your grain a lot of flavour too. They were made to play around with so experiment with whatever is to hand. The worst that can happen is that either you can undercook them – pretend you did it on purpose: "Al dente" – or you overcook them, but that's okay too, it just means it's a bit soggy, but that's not the end of the world.

You can add almost anything to rice. At one end of the scale is good old plain rice, and at the other end is a risotto, where the whole meal happens in the one pot. If you want one-pot rice 'n vegetables, simply chop the veg up into small pieces and add them to the boiling water, stir and follow the instructions for simple rice. What you're doing is using the same water to cook both ingredients, that's all. The general point is that the harder the vegetable and the stronger the flavour the longer it needs to cook for. Onions and garlic for example, should be fried first, before the rice is added whereas say, bamboo shoots or tomatoes can be dropped in much later.

Rice is great with finely chopped carrots, courgettes and mushrooms or with peppers, onions and garlic. Spices also work well and should be added to onions that have been fried for about 5 minutes.

You can also go for a slightly different flavour by adding nuts, raisins or

sultanas. Cashew nuts dropped into the water at the same time as the rice become deliciously juicy, and almonds – especially if you have boiled them for ten minutes, slipped off their skins, then fried them with orange zest – are just divine. Bringing the milk from a coconut to the boil and stirring that into cooked rice also has delicious results, as does putting in some desiccated coconut.

The more things you add, the more the rice becomes a meal in its own right. When this happens, you have a risotto. I've included a basic recipe from which you can add whatever takes your fancy.

As a general rule, 1 cup or ½ mug or one and bit handfuls of dry rice is enough for one, hungryish backpacker. About twice as much water as rice.

SIMPLE RICE:

Rice, Water, Salt

Bring the water to the boil, add some salt then the rice, stir. Let it bubble and top it up with water if the level gets a little low. The rice should always be well covered with boiling liquid. Normally, it will take about 20-25 minutes to cook. Keep an eye on it and stir occasionally. It doesn't need a lid. If you are using brown rice, it will take longer. Drain well and serve. For perfect breakfast rice, when it's cooked simply roughly drain it and then press it down in the pot and put a lid on. Eat it ten minutes later with your hands!

GRAINS RECIPES

FLUFFY RICE:

Basmati or other long-grained rice, Water, Salt, Oil

Put the rice you want to eat into something like a mug or a bowl. Make a mental note of the level that it reaches. Put the rice in your pot and then in the same mug or bowl as you measured the rice, measure one and a half times the amount of water. Keep the water to the side. Fry the grains for about a minute, then add the water to your pot.. Put the lid on and bring the water to the boil. You need to let it bubble gently for about 15-20 minutes. If you're cooking on a stove, turn down the heat, otherwise move the pot to a cooler part of your grate, but if you can't change the heat don't worry too much. The steam should be sneaking out from under the lid. Keep the lid on, and resisting the temptation to peek (you need the steam for the fluffiness) leave it to one side, off the heat, for 5-10 minutes. Give the rice a quick stir and it's ready.

If you can't get Basmati or other thin-grained rice, you'll need to fry the rice for a bit longer first to stop it from sticking to its next-door neighbour. Two minutes of quick frying with a little bit of oil or fat is enough. If you find that it's a bit too sticky, next time you make it, during those last 5 minutes shake it about, and run a fork through it a few times – this will help it dry evenly.

Risotto

Onion, Rice, Oil/Margarine/Butter/Fat, Water & stock cube/stock (you need about twice as much water as rice), Optional Extras (perhaps some meat or other veg or nuts)

Cut the onion and chopped meat (if you're using it) into smallish pieces. Put in the pan with oil sear them until everything is golden. This will take about 5 to 7 minutes. Add the dry rice and stir it all around for a further 2 minutes or so then add about a third of the water. Keep stirring so that nothing sticks to the pan. When the rice has absorbed the water, add the next third. When it's absorbed this, it will be almost done. Add more liquid – don't use it all if you don't have to. Stir it all in, taste the rice to make sure it's to your liking, and then take it off the heat and cover it until you want to eat it. Season with salt and pepper. You can replace the last third of water with white or red wine if there's some around. Ideally, you'd add some grated cheese just before serving.

If you want to replace the meat with seafood or fish, that should be cooked first. All you then need to do is warm it up by adding it at the last stage. To cook seafood and fish see p. 24 to p. 31.

Recommended variations include adding: pork and cooked lentils and peppers; saffron, white wine and parsley; chicken and mushroom; seafood and chilli; beans and herbs; orange, nuts and raisins (add the juice of a couple of oranges at almost the very end).

Bulghar

Bulghur is cracked wheat grain and has a special nutty taste. It's so simple to use, all you do is cover it in cold water and leave it for about 15 minutes. Give it a squeeze and it is ready to use. It works very well as part of a salad – say tomatoes, onions and lemon juice.

Cous Cous

Cous cous, Water, Knob of butter or splodge of oil (if there is some)

Cous Cous can be cooked in lots of ways: in the oven, steamed or soaked – the backpacker's way is to soak it. Bring some water, milk or a mix of both (maybe an inch or so) to the boil in your pot and drop in the butter or oil of you have it. Add slightly less cous cous than there is water. Take the pot off the heat. Cover and leave for about 10 – 15 minutes. You don't need to drain it, the cous cous should absorb all the water. If it's still a bit too hard, add a bit more boiling water.

To liven things up, first fry other ingredients (such as nuts, fruit or spices) and then pour the water that is to be boiled on top of them. Raw, finely chopped carrots, raw mushrooms, raw peppers, raw thinly sliced onions, any edible herbs can also be added to the cous cous once it's cooked. Sultanas can be added into the boiling water at the same time as the cous cous to great effect. You might also like to try adding some fennel or caraway seeds to the water and then squeezing a lime over the cous cous just before serving.

Polenta - Posho - Cornmeal - Grits - Semolina

In Britain, maize only tends to be eaten as 'corn on the cob', there's nothing wrong with that – it's delicious. Bright and yellow, people often do not realise that it comes in white as well, and is eaten all over the world. Ground down yellow maize is known in Italy as polenta, and in Africa white maize is known by many names including Ugali, Milli, Posho and even polenta. The flour is dry and powdery so your job, if you want to eat it, is to get some water absorbed.

Note: If you're in Italy or elsewhere in Europe, you might come across Polenta in a packet. It might be instant or slow cooking so the best thing is to follow the instructions on the box. In most of other parts of the world, you'll just get the flour in a plastic bag from a street vendor or farmer.

A dollop of polenta or posho on the side of a plate makes a perfect accompaniment to vegetables or meat. You can give yourself a more fashionable supper by cutting a slice of polenta and putting it on the barbecue: the charring from the great looks magnificent. Put it on your plate with lots of black pepper and then put whatever sauce you want on the top. You can also make a tower by putting one layer of polenta, one of meat or veg, another layer of polenta and then more meat or veg, pouring sauce over the whole thing and around the side of the plate.

GROUND GRAINS

Water, Salt, Oil or butter (optional), Finely chopped vegetables (optional)

Bring a pot of salted water, about ½ full to the boil. At this point add some oil or butter if you have it, so that you have a globule in the middle of the pan. Add finely chopped vegetables if you want to. Let this bubble and fizz away for another couple of minutes then slowly add, stirring all the time, the flour. The basic point is to stir it so that there are no lumps. The thickness of the Polenta/posho will depend on how much water is in your pot, and how much flour you have added. You know that you have added enough when it is thick slowly bubbling like an erupting hot yellow or white mud bath. Be exceptionally careful not to get scalded. You need to leave it for about half an hour on a lower heat. You have to keep stirring it, otherwise it will stick to the bottom of the pot. It is done when it's gets very thick, and has started to come away from the side of the pot. Spoon it out and serve.

In Uganda, it's normally served thick and dry. To get this effect, just leave it on the heat for another five or so minutes – you'll have a hard job stirring it so just try to keep the heat quite low so that the bottom doesn't burn. If you've got leftovers (which is highly likely as no one ever seems able to finish a plate of this stuff!), slice it into pieces and pop it on the bbq for a few minutes either side – it'll char nicely.

PULSES

Pulses, I confess, isn't really a word that gets your mouth watering or your pulse racing, for that matter. I'm sure the Black-Eyed Peas wouldn't have had half their success if they were called "the last subgroup of the staple category". Use them as part of a soup, stew or salad. They all give texture, colour and a boost of protein to your meal.

Pulses are also backpacker friendly because they last for ages and are virtually indestructible. An extra bonus is that they are really social: you buy them by the bagful at a market and, like rice, you'll need to go through them, bean by bean, taking out the stones and any dodgy-looking ones. I made some great pals on a very long trip down the river Congo. Sorting our beans kept us occupied for hours.

Think white beans, red beans, black beans, giant beans, chick peas, lentils. Most beans you will normally find will be dried so, as always, you need to get some water in them to soften them up and bring out the flavours. Soaking them in unsalted cold water overnight greatly reduces the cooking time and should be done for most big pulses. The next day, rinse them off, pour some unsalted water over the top, bring to the boil and simmer. On average, it will take about an hour to cook, but try one and see, the older the bean, the longer it will take. A good hint is not to add salt to the water as it toughens them up. Putting a peeled potato and a scored tomato in will help to soften the skins of the pulses.

DAAL/LENTILS

Lentils, Garlic or Onions, Salt, Spices (Turmeric, Cumin, Coriander, anything), Oil

Soak the lentils for a few hours then wash and drain. Boil some slightly salty water and add the lentils. Cook gently for 30 mins then add the spices. In a frying pan, add chopped onions and/or garlic to some hot oil. When these have browned

pour the oil mixture over the simmering lentils. Cover and cook for another 5 minutes. Great with rice or bread.

HUMMUS

Chickpeas (cooked), Lemon, Oil, Garlic (or onions/shallots/spring onions)

Smash the garlic, get the rind off the lemon, slice it thinly and squeeze out the juice. Smash the cooked chickpeas with a fork and mix in a bit of the lemon and garlic. Keep going until you have enough to eat and you have a flavour that you like.

PORTABLE LIVE SPROUTING SALAD

unsplit lentils, chick peas, alfalfa seeds, small beans

A great way to make sure you always have fresh salad is to grow your own. Use a simple clear screw-topped jam jar. Throw enough lentils or beans in to cover the bottom, add just enough water to cover them and put the lid on to keep the moisture in. After a few days the beans will start to sprout. Change the water every day and shake the jar to make sure the beans stay moist. Strap your jars to the outside of your backpack so they get enough light. Soon you will have a jar full of extremely tasty and nutritious bean and lentil salad – all you need to survive!

Meat and Fish - Fish

Cooking meat or fish is sometimes seen as prohibitively difficult – we worry that we won't cook it right and will make ourselves ill. In many cases that's a well-founded fear because it's dodgy meat that makes most people ill on holiday. But that's no reason to avoid it altogether: cooking it yourself is the best way of being sure that it's good. You buy good stuff, then you cook it right. By far the most important thing is to buy fresh. Look out for a couple of things: for fish, look first at the eyes. They shouldn't be gluey or hazy but should look as they did when the fish was alive, this tells you that the fish is fresh and that it has not been stored under the sun; secondly, the flesh should be firm and the scales or skin shiny. If it whiffs, leave it well alone.

As far as meat is concerned, look to buy from somewhere where the meat is not kept in the sun. Next you need to use your fingers if you can, press the meat – fresh stuff will respond by either seeping blood, or watery liquid – if it feels or looks dry or hard, forget it. Again, use your nose and avoid smelly stuff. Once you've bought your meat, clean it and wash off dust, grime and grit. Keep it covered and in the shade, or in the fridge if you've got access to one, until you use it. Cooking meat and fish is easy. It's all about keeping an eye on it to make sure it's not over or under done. Try it!

Fish and Shellfish

It's the ultimate night: on the beach ... fresh fish that was caught just out to sea ... a good fire ... fantastic.

Fish tastes great on its own, but it's good to have some staples on the side, and it's also well worth adding some extra zing to the fish from time to time. As far as the zing is concerned, my top tip is any tropical fruit: stuff it with mangos

and bananas, steam it with sliced kiwi and serve with passion fruit, anything will work. Also fantastic is nuts: try fish with blanched, flaked or crushed nuts, almonds particularly. This gives a welcome change in texture. Spices are great too, but don't just shake some curry powder over the fish, get inventive: make a paste with finely chopped onions, add to that some coconut milk or creamed coconut, mix in the spices and add some black pepper; salsas work well, especially when the fish has been fried – mix finely chopped onion, tomatoes, chillies with lime juice, oil and bit of sugar and pour it over the fish.

Your staple will, of course, vary depending on what is available. Fish is delicious served on a bed of rice. The rice can be plain, or flavoured in any of the ways described earlier, especially coconut rice. When you're poaching fish, try serving it with mashed potato. Fried fish is good with some salad – even just a tomato and a few bits of onion. The ultimate is to roast a pineapple and to use that as a receptacle from which to eat the deboned fish – divine.

When you're doing prawns, or other shellfish, it is really simple to make a little sauce to serve them in. Start with your base of onions, maybe garlic and spices, then add the shellfish. Fry them off and then add some tomatoes, or some fruit, or some white wine.

Preparing a Fish

If the fish has scales (you'll know because you get left with scales on your hands when you pick it up) scrape them off with a knife – it's best to hold the tail and do it in a downwards motion. Next, with your sharpest knife, make a deep slit in the underside of the fish lengthways from head to tail. Scoop and pull out all the insides with your fingers and discard them. The best thing is to burn them on your fire – otherwise they'll attract loads of flies. Cut off any top or side fins and burn them too. Give the inside of the fish a good rinse with some water making sure that the blood and veiny bits are cleaned away, then rinse the outside of the fish too. It's ready to cook. If you've got a thing about bones, you should fillet the fish. To do this, lay it on its side on a stable, flat surface and slice, as close as the backbone as possible, from tail to head. If you haven't got a very, very sharp knife then there's no point even trying this. Once you've got the fillet, check for any small bones, carefully pulling out those you come across. If the fish is small, like anchovies say, no knife is needed as you can just pull the head and spine away from the body.

FLESHY FISH ON THE BARBECUE

Fish, Oil or butter (optional)

I think this is the best way to eat fish. Prepare the fish, then with a sharp knife make three slashes on either side. Run some oil on one side of the fish, or smear it with butter and then put that side on the grate. After some time, turn it over. It will take roughly 15 – 20 minutes depending on the size of the fish and the heat from your fire. Take it off and its ready to eat. Don't forget the skin, crisp and burnt – it's the best bit.

Fillets can be smeared with oil and cooked for 4 minutes on each side. If it's a thin fillet from an oily fish, like mackerel you can thread it onto a skewer, pop a wedge of onion on each end and barbecue them for 10 – 12 minutes.

SQUID ON THE BARBECUE

Squid, Citrus

If you can get squid that has already been gutted and cleaned, that's great, if not, then you'll have to do it yourself. Take the squid and with a very sharp knife cut open the body and scrape out the guts. Chop off the eyes and mouth but leave the tentacles together in their bunch. Lay the body out flat and using a knife make criss cross incisions all over the body. Rinse it well and put it on the grate and press it down. Turn it over once. It is ready in 1 or 2 minutes – as soon as it starts to curl up. If there are baby squid around, you can chop off the head and tentacles, clean it out and then stuff the body with anything you like (cooked rice with vegetables or fruit say) and using a thin clean twig, fasten the top shut and then put it on the grate for four minutes or so, turning regularly. Give it a good squeeze of citrus, anything – lemon, lime, grapefruit, and eat it while it's piping hot. Don't worry if the squid is chewy, it's supposed to be.

SHELLFISH SKEWERS

Shellfish, Skewers

Don't be surprised when you buy some prawns and they are greyish blue and not pink – that's how they come. Clean them thoroughly, cut off the heads if you want, then skewer them and cook on the barbecue for about four minutes, turning regularly.

If you've got something big enough not to fall through the grate, say langoustines, put them straight on the grate for 3 minutes either side. If you've got anything bigger – like a crab or lobster, it's best to boil it (see p. 30).

STEAMED FISH

Fish, Leaves

Sometimes, it's fun to stuff a fish or to cook it with things on top. Cooking a stuffed fish straight on the grate is too tricky so the best thing is to steam it. Get some large fresh leaves (but don't refuse tin foil if there is some!): banana leaves work well, as do the leafy bits that are on the edge of maize cobs – any leafy fleshy thing will do. Prepare the fish, stuff it with something or just pour or place your mix on top of the fish, don't worry about cutting off the head and tail, and wrap it up in the leaf as tight as you can. Don't wrap it up too much, about two layers of leaf is perfect. Put in your grate or in your grilling unit and leave it for about 20 minutes or so. If your leaves start to really burn away, just move the fish to a cooler part of the fire.

If you're not near to leaves, you can add this stuff to the fish once it's been cooked on the barbecue. The flavours don't infuse as much, but it will still taste good.

FRIED FISH

Fish, Flour, Water or Milk, Butter/oil, Salt & pepper, Spices & herbs (optional)

Spread some flour (plain or cornflour) out on a flat surface, and season it with salt and pepper, take your prepared fish which you have wet slightly with milk or some water, and lay one side and then the other on the flour. Tap off any excess flour and sprinkle on any herbs or spices that you might have. Put it in a pot with some already hot butter or oil and fry it until it is golden and the flesh is tender and opaque, this will take about 5 minutes on each side, depending on the fish and the heat from your fire. Don't move the fish too much for the first few minutes or the flour will come off.

If you're frying squid, prepare it as above (p. 17), follow these same steps but only cook it for thirty seconds.

Fried Shellfish

Shellfish, Flour, Oil, Herbs or spices (optional)

Scallops, oysters, get whatever you've got out of it shell by inserting a knife close to the hinge and prising it open. Rinse the flesh, trim off any hard bits and pat them dry. They're ready to fry. Put them in a hot oiled pot for one minute, turn them over and cook for another couple of minutes keeping them moving. If you like, you can add something aromatic to the pot or you can lightly dust them in flour to make them a bit crispy.

For prawns and the like, these need to be seared. After rinsing them, put them in a pan with some hot oil of fat. No lid. They are done when they turn pink, which is about 6 – 9 minutes later, depending on size.

LOBSTER

Lobsters should be dropped head first, alive, into a pot of furiously boiling, salted water with a lid on for about 10 minutes for a lobster that is big enough to feed two people. If you've got a soft spot for our pincered pal, you can make him sleep by covering him in a damp cloth. Drop him into the pot and by the time he wakes up, well, he won't wake up.

Once it's cooked, let it stand for about five minutes. You need to take out the yucky bits so put your knife just behind its eyes and split the front and then split it open along its entire length. You can now take out the stomach, the gills and the dark vein running down the tail.

FISH COOKED IN WATER

Fish. Water or Milk (or a mix of both)

Poaching a fish doesn't only mean going and nicking it from a local landowner, it's also cooking the fish in water. This can be quite tricky for the backpacker because the water needs to be at a certain temperature – not boiling hard but gently, hardly simmering. It's easier to do if you have a portable stove, a large grate with cooler parts or a few extra stones to increase the distance between the pot and the flames. It's worth it too, the end result is very different from fried or barbecued fish, much more soothing and homely.

Prepare the fish and bring a pot of water, milk or a mix of both, (which can have salt, herbs or strong flavoured vegetables in it if you want) to the point where it is simmering and little bubbles are forming on the bottom of the pot and rising the surface. Gently put the fish in and leave it to cook, turning it once only. Cooking time will depend on the fish but it should be about four or five minutes on either side – you'll know it's done when you can slide a piece from the flesh. Take it out carefully and serve.

SHELLFISH COOKED IN WATER

Shellfish (here Mussels), Water, White wine (optional)

Clean them very carefully, scraping off all hairy, scary bits so that you are just left with nice clean shells. Discard any that are open. Put them in a pot with an inch of boiling, salted water, cover tightly, leave for about 4 minutes until they've opened. Discard any that stay closed. You can give them a bit more flavour by frying an onion and some garlic adding a little bit of water then the mussels. White wine is always great, if there is some, pour in a few glugs instead of water.

MARINATED FISH

Very very fresh Fish (fleshy or shelly), Citrus juice, Salt, Pepper (corns if possible) Spring onion/Onion/garlic/shallots – finely chopped

Cut your fish into thin thin slices. Mix the rest of the ingredients together and pour the mixture over the fish and leave for about 45 minutes. Serve up and squeeze some more lemon over the top.

DRIED FISH

Quite often, you come across dried fish. It doesn't taste that great but if you do want to cook it, all you do is soak it for a day, changing the water three or four times to get rid of the saltiness then cook it any manner described above – it works well in soup.

MEAT

You know what I'm going to say, don't you? Cooking meat is easy. The basic idea is, as always, to get some heat inside the meat. You can do this on the barbecue or in the pot. Meat doesn't need much in the way of preparation, just make sure that it's clean, and you're all set!

MEAT ON THE BARBECUE

Meat, Oil/fat (if needed)

This is my favourite way to cook meat. Cooking times will vary depending on which type and which cut of meat you're using as well as the thickness of the piece, the heat of the coals and whether you like it well-done, medium, or rare. Turn the meat once or twice during cooking. Use this table as a rough guide:

Beef Steak	Rare – 5 mins
	Medium – 8 mins
	Well Done – 12 mins
Lamb Steak/Chops	10-15 mins
Pork Steak/Chops	10-15 mins
Chicken Quarters	30-35 mins
Boneless Breasts	10-15 mins
Drumsticks	25-30 mins

Kebabs are also fun. Dice the meat into pieces about two fingers by two fingers. Thread your meat onto a soaked skewer and cook it for anything from 10-15 minutes depending on how hot the fire is and how big the pieces are.

Marinades

Marinating meat is a great thing to do as it helps make it juicier and adds character. I always rely on my backpacker's marinade: oil, garlic, black pepper. Put the meat in your pot a few hours before cooking time, making sure that it is in a single layer, add the marinade not forgetting to use loads of squashed garlic, and make sure that everything is coated evenly. Turn the meat from time to time. You can add chillies too if you have them. A different alternative is just to use fruit – either as a marinade, or just as something serve alongside: try kiwi and lamb, orange and chicken, or beef and banana.

FRIED MEAT

Meat, Oil/fat/butter/margarine

Prepare the meat. Put it in hot oil and fry it until it's done. The time taken will vary enormously depending on what you're cooking, how hot the oil is and how thick the pieces of meat are. The key thing is to make sure that it is cooked all of the way through. You can add spices or herbs to the oil as you fry the meat.

STEAMED MEAT

Meat, Water

Put a little bit of water in the bottom of your pot, not very much, just about half a centimetre deep. When this is bubbling vigorously, drop your meat in and put a lid on. Let them sit there with a lid on and move them around occasionally making sure that they don't stick to the bottom. By the time that the water has evaporated away the meat should be cooked. This is only a rough a ready rule and if the meat is thick it will take a bit longer and you'll need to add more water.

Stew

Meat, Oil/fat/butter/margarine or water, Onions and/or Garlic, other ingredients

Prepare the meat and dice it into 2 finger by 2 finger-sized pieces. Fry the onions and garlic, with any herbs or spices that you might be adding then add the meat. Fry it, or steam it, whatever you prefer. Add any other vegetables that you might have and then add water, enough so that it's covered twice over. Let it cook: allow about ½ hour per pound (one full heaped hand of fresh meat will weight about a pound). You can use beer or wine instead of some – or up to half if you want it boozy – of the water.

There are literally hundreds of variations of stews, you need to be guided by what is around. Use nuts if they are around, put in peanut butter, put in herbs, spices, any roots, pulses or fruit. Go for it.

You can the serve it up, either on its own, with salad, staples, or bread, whatever you have. Some of my favourites are:

Beef in Beer with Onion and Root; Lamb with Red Wine, Berries and Herbs; Chicken and Curried Vegetables; Pork in Peanut Butter; Pork and Fruit (apricot is my all time favourite).

Steak Tartare

Finest Beef, Onion, an Egg

This one is only for you if, first, you have access to top quality, superfresh beef, and second, you are the kind of person (rather you than me, but each to their own) that actually will take pleasure in eating a raw burger.

Mince the steak or, if you don't have a mincer chop it up as finely as you can. Add a very finely chopped onion, salt and pepper, and then mix it all together. If you are going all out, crack a raw egg on top and then it's all set to eat.

Eggs

Eggs are universally available and versatile too. You are more likely to find a good egg if you follow a couple of tips. Number one, don't buy eggs that are on display in the sun. Number two, only buy eggs that have shells that are all one colour if there are any dark or clear patches on the shell steer clear. If there are hens pecking around and it's a busy market, it's likely that they'll be fresh.

Soft-Boiled Egg

Egg, Water

Add the egg to a pot of simmering water – slide it in on a spoon rather than plop it in – bring the water back to the boil and cover and leave for around three minutes. If the egg cracks – it should only do this if you've plopped it in the water or if it has come out of the fridge, not likely – add a couple of good pinches of salt to the water.

Omelettes

Eggs, Oil/Fat

Stir three eggs together with a fork, but don't make them fluffy. Add this to your pot in which the base is covered by sizzling oil/fat. Leave it for a minute, then scrape it with a fork so that the uncooked eggs run through to the bottom. When the top is still soft – not runny – tip it out onto a plate and serve.

There are so many varieties of omelette – your only limit is your imagination. The only thing to remember is that whatever you put in has to be cooked by the time you eat it. That means roots will need to be precooked, as will meat, fish or onions, garlic, aubergines etc.

HARD-BOILED EGG

Egg, Water

Put the egg in a pot of cold water. Bring it to the boil and cook for around ten minutes from the moment the water boils. Sprinkle salt and pepper before you eat.

POACHED EGG

Egg, Water

Bring a pot of water to a gentle simmer. Crack your egg into a bowl, mug or anything except the pot. Tip the egg into the water and don't touch it. Leave it like that for three minutes. If you want a firmer yolk, pop a lid on the pot.

SCRAMBLED EGG

Egg, Milk/Butter, Oil/fat

Beat some eggs in a bowl together with a splash of milk and/or melted butter. Allow two or three per backpacker. Get a pot hot. add some oil, then add the eggs. Stir, and don't stop. This is best done over a low heat, so it your fire is very hot, take the pot off now and again to cool it down. Keep stirring, scraping the bottom, of the pot After about five ten minutes the eggs will be starting to harden. Serve them up asap.

SAUCES AND SOUPS

There is something about sauces and soups that is really comforting. It's a homely, warming thing. I love them. Plus they're a doddle to make and have infinite variations. The secret is this: at the heart of every good sauce or soup is an onion. Fry one, gently if possible, until it is just starting to go translucent, and from there the world is your oyster. You can make some sauce and pour it over meat or vegetables or cook the vegetables or meat in liquid as a 'sauce', 'stew' or 'soup'. The principles are very simple: make a base of strongly flavoured ingredients and add the meat and then later the liquid

BASIC SOUP

Onion, Water, other vegetables or meat

For me, the best soups, apart from starting with a fried onion, all have a root of one sort or another in them. They give it body, and make it hearty and filling. Root soup alone alone, however, is bland bland bland. It needs something to give it flavour. This is where the veggies come in. You can go for it big time. Use any vegetable. The only rule is that you fry it off for five minutes or so with the onion. This is to bring out the flavour and avoid that boiled vegetable taste.

Once you've done that, add the chopped, peeled root, cover it with water, bring it to the boil, and leave it to simmer. When the root, or the meat if you have used it, has cooked right through, you can either serve it straight or mash it into as smooth a pulp as your fork will allow.

Some of my favourite soups are made by mixing vegetables from the onion family, like leeks, garlic, shallots etc with roots like potato, celeriac or sweet potatoes. Simple soups generally tends to be the most successful.

Basic Tomato Sauce

Oil, Onion (and Garlic if available), Tomatoes, A little water

Heat up some oil in your pot. and add a couple of crushed and chopped garlic cloves and the onion. Fry these for a few minutes. If you are making a meat sauce, add the meat at this point and cook it until it is browned (about four minutes depending on how thick you've cut the pieces and how hot your fire is). Next add the chopped tomatoes and then a little water – just enough to almost come to the level of the tomatoes. Let this simmer away for about ten minutes, or until the meat is cooked all the way through. Add more water if you find it's bubbling away to nothing. To get Italian, add some herbs, bay leaves or oregano. You can also spice it up with some curry powder or ground spices.

VEGETABLES

The colour, texture and flavours are what make vegetables great. Making a fabulous meal is really simple but still, most backpackers, including me for years, make the mistake of boiling them. Boiled vegetables taste dull and lifeless. Boiling is boring. Boiling steals the flavours and deadens the texture of any vegetable. Pop them on the grate instead and it's a different experience – the skin gets blackened in places, the juices stay inside and dribble down your chin when you take a bite. The flavours become deep and rich and grate-cooked vegetables are just as good eaten cold the next day. Or whack them in a pan for a quick sweat or stir-fry so that they get hot and their flavours mingle slightly. Or eat them raw, on their own or in a salad, and savour the colours and the taste. Just don't serve a plate of plain soft-boiled carrots.

Barbecued vegetables go with anything, but work best with staples that are slightly more moist, such as risotto (add the vegetables just as the last third of water is being added), mashed roots, pulses, polenta, cous cous, or bulghur.

As far as serving them up is concerned, don't just serve them on the side, chop them up and stir them in, or make a tower from, say, one layer cold polenta, one layer of a particular vegetable, another layer of polenta and then more of a different vegetable. Whoever said playing with your food was silly? It's art baby!

BARBECUED VEGETABLES

Vegetables, Oil/Fat, Salt and pepper

Most large vegetables can simply be put straight onto the grate. The principle is the same as always: get some heat inside. Cooking times will vary on the thickness

of the vegetable and how moist it is. For example, an aubergine can be cooked whole (turned quite often) and will take about 30 minutes. A thin slice will be done in a few minutes. A tomato will be done very quickly.

Dryer vegetables should have some oil, butter or fat smeared on to them. Extra flavour can be gained by seasoning the vegetables with salt and pepper, and adding any herbs or spices that you might have to hand. You can also give them a good squeeze of citrus just before you eat them. There's no need to overdo it with the frills though, a onion quarter, barbecued, oily and hot needs nothing more than a good scattering of salt to make it heavenly.

KEBABS

Vegetables – cut into bite size chunks, Oil / Fat, Salt & Pepper, Skewers soaked in water, Meat/Fish (optional)

Vegetables were made to be skewered. A plain vegetable kebab can be made from anything, mushrooms, tomatoes, onions, courgettes. The principle is to cut them into chunks or wedges and put some oil or fat on them if you have it. If you add some root or banana it should have been par-boiled for a short while first. Meat should have, if possible, been marinated (see p. 33) so that it becomes more tender.

A sweet and sour kebab, asking to be served on a bed of plain rice, can be made from a peppers (preferably green and yellow), quartered tomato, cauliflower or broccoli and pineapple. You can brush them with some oil, lemon and, if you have them, honey and chilli sauce. They will need about ten minutes or so to cook. You can enhance the flavours of things on your skewer by wrapping them in something aromatic, say mint or basil – whatever is to hand.

PATTIES

Onion, Garlic (optional but nice), Cooked pulses (mashed with a fork if needed), finely chopped Mushrooms (about twice as much as the onions and garlic), Flour

The principle for a vegetable pattie is the same as for a potato pattie: get something arranged into a burger shape and either fry it or put it on the barbecue.

Fry the onion and garlic in your pot until they have softened, add some spices if you have them and fry for another minute. Add the chopped mushrooms and cook for about five more minutes. Take the pot off the heat and let it cool (or transfer the mixture to a big bowl if you have one). Add the pulses handful by handful mixing with your fingers. Keep adding until the mixture reaches a consistency where you can make it into a patty shape. Put some flour on your hands and make the patties. Smear on some oil or fat and fry them for 8 to 10 minutes, turning once, or carefully put them on the barbecue for the same amount of time. You can replace the mushrooms with any chopped vegetable you like but remember, if the mixture is too wet, mix in some flour to dry it up.

Stir-Fried Vegetables

Vegetables cut into thin pieces, Oil/Fat (just a little), Salt & Pepper, Meat cut into thin strips or fish (optional)

Take a selection of vegetables, say carrots, mushrooms, greens, courgettes and slice them thinly. Heat up some oil or fat in a pan (add some ginger or lemongrass or anything aromatic if you have it) and add your vegetables all in one go, stir gently, making sure that nothing catches for about five minutes. You won't have a wok with you, so you'll need to keep things moving to stop them from burning. Serve as it is, with salt and pepper or a squidge of citrus. You could add some cooked rice, thinly sliced meat (but brown it before stirring in the vegetables), or cooked fish if you like. You can pour honey over vegetables too if you like.

Juicy vegetables

Vegetables, Garlic (optional but makes a big difference), Oil/Fat, Salt & Pepper

Skewered vegetables do lose some of their juices. You can avoid this by chopping the vegetables as if to be skewered and putting them in your pot to form a single layer. Dribble a bit of oil over everything, add some salt and pepper and lots of squashed garlic cloves and leave on the barbecue or stove, stirring once in a while to make sure nothing sticks, for about 25 minutes or 'till are starting to get a lovely char on the outside.

Raw vegetables

The vegetables you will buy as a backpacker will tend to have been produced locally and non-intensively. Make the most of it. You'll find that they have much more flavour than those at home, and will often not need to be cooked at all. Munch on a carrot, courgette or tomato as you walk, don't overlook garlic cloves either. Just make sure you wash them first.

COOKED GREENS *(That means anything green and leafy)*

Boiled greens just taste foul. Don't do it. They can be fried or, in the case of very fine leaved, delicate greens like spinach, dumped in a pot still wet from being rinsed with a lid for a minute or so. Get the greens into equal sized shreds or strips and put them in a pot with a little hot oil at the bottom. Heat them, stirring so that nothing sticks, until they turn deep green – that's it. You'll know if you've done them too long as they will taste bitter.

You can vary the flavour with salt, or by adding things with strong flavours to the oil: use whatever is to hand – chopped garlic, ginger, chillies, ground or chopped nuts. They work with a squeeze of citrus on top too.

COB IN WATER

Maize cob, Water, Salt & pepper, Butter/margarine (optional)

Put the cleaned, de-leaved cob in a pot of cold water (if it doesn't fit, chop or break it in half) and bring it to the boil for about ten minutes. Take it off the heat and by the time the water is cool it should be ready. Take it out, sprinkle some pepper on and then smear some butter over the top just before you eat it.

COB ON THE BARBECUE

Maize cob with leaves on

Clean the cob but keep on a layer of leaves and place it straight on your grate. Turn occasionally and by the time the leaf has burnt through and the kernels are nice and charred, it's ready to eat.

46

AVOCADO

Cut one in half, take out the stone (if you thread it onto one of your spare skewers, and balance that on a tin can filled with water, it will grow. Plant it and start a little garden) and eat them as they are, no salt or pepper – delicious.

If the avocado is quite hard, you can cut in half and lay it on a hot barbecue, still with its skin on, for a couple of minutes on the flesh side, and then about 5 minutes on the skin side. Add salt and pepper and enjoy it.

GUACAMOLE

Avocados, Garlic, Onion, Chillies (if they are around), Lemon juice

Half the avocado and scoop the insides into a pot, mash them with a fork until smoothish. Finely chop the onion, garlic and chilli and stir them in. Squeeze the lemon juice on the top and stir that in too. Eat straight away (it won't keep).

AVOCADO SAUCES

The texture of sauces made from avocado lend a creamy, almost mayonnaise-like quality to things. Cut them in half, take out the stone, scoop out the flesh – don't forget that you can use the empty skin as a receptacle from which to serve your gourmet style sauce! Now you can mix whatever you want with the avocado – try anything. Sweetcorn (scraped from a cob that you have earlier cooked on the barbecue) will give you an exciting texture; orange juice and finely sliced orange zest will give you a lighter sauce that goes well with any Staple and is great spooned on fish or chicken; mashed beans and lime are just great as well. It's up to you!

SALADS

The dictionary calls a salad a 'cold mixture of usu. raw vegetables, often with a dressing'. With definitions like that, it's no wonder that some backpacker's salads are simply dull old sliced tomatoes. A better definition would be 'cold or warm vegetables or fruits, sliced, diced, trimmed, slimmed, mashed, smashed, cored or scored'. The only thing is that, as you are not cooking anything you need to make sure you wash all ingredients carefully first.

MATCHSTICK SALAD

Vegetables, Fruit, Garlic, Citrus, 2 pinches of sugar, Chillies (optional), Salt & pepper

Crush some garlic and squeeze the citrus zest over it and stir in the sugar. If you have chillies, you can add them too – chopped up small. Shave the rind off the citrus and cut it into thin, thin matchstick strips and add them to the garlic mix. Next, slice your crunchy or soft vegetables (say carrots and courgettes or cucumber) into thin, thin matchstick strips. Do the same with some fruit, mango, banana, guava anything. Put everything in a bowl then pour the garlic citrus mix over the top. Season to taste.

CRUNCHY SALAD

Crunchy fruit, Crunchy vegetables, Lemon, Salt, Sugar, Oil, Mustard (optional), Salt & pepper

Core and cut the crunchy fruit into slices and squeeze some lemon juice over them. Cut the crunchy vegetables (celery, fennel bulb, chicory, radishes etc) into thin slices. Mix a bit of oil with salt, sugar, mustard and maybe a bit of something alcoholic if you have it. Dribble this over the fruit and vegetables. Season to taste.

Chewy salad

Vegetables, Fruit, Nuts, Raisins, Citrus, Salt & pepper

Cut whatever vegetables you have into small chunks (grated carrots are the ultimate). Add any leafy things that you might have. Add fruit, chopped nuts and raisins. Squeeze some citrus over the top and season to taste.

MOUTH MELTING SALAD

Soft fruit, Soft vegetabl

Cut your soft vegetables (like mushrooms or tomatoes) into manageable pieces and do the same for the soft fruit (melon, papaya etc). Squeeze a bit of lemon juice over the top and season to taste.

WARM SALAD

Vegetables, Fruit, Root, Meat/fish, Salt and pepper

Chop up the vegetables and fruit as you want. Add some boiled root to which you have added salt and pepper and then meat or fish. Add mustard or any dressing that you can come up with. Season to taste.

HERBS AND SPICES

Herbs and spices are also a really useful secret weapon for backpackers when faced with limited ingredients. A few pinches of this or that any can drastically alter the taste of your meal. I once only had access to cabbage, onion, and tomato for more or less two months (no, I wasn't in prison). It wasn't the highest point of my culinary career, but with a store cupboard of curry powder, pepper, dried chillies, and fennel seeds, I managed to get quite a lot of variety out of just three ingredients.

Store herbs as airtight as possible, plus out of the sun and away from the heat. They should easily keep for the duration of your trip. When cooking, the rule for fresh herbs is the tougher they are, the earlier they go in your pot. The spectrum ranges from woody things like rosemary which can be added right at the start, to basil or parsley, which should be added right at the end, or else they will just dissolve and wilt away.

Dried herbs are much more hardy. You can add them to the food from the very beginning, or, if you're feeling 'haut' or simply because you're not keen on picking bits of herbs out of your gums, you can make a *bouquet garni*: put some herbs onto a clean, small cloth, say the size of a hanky, and then tie it up tightly at the top. You can then drop this straight into your stew, sauce, meat or whatever and you're all set to infuse.

Using spice: Whole spices that are seeds, like cardamon, can be toasted before using to bring out the flavour. It's easy, just pop them in a pot, without oil, stir them all around for a few minutes until you catch the whiff of spice and then they're ready to add. Ground spice is strong, so you don't need much at all to deliver a big result. You can add it early on in the cooking process, or you can sprinkle it directly on the food at the end – say banana with a cinnamon dusting!

AFTERS

I'm a pudding maniac. Can't get enough. One of the highlights for me of going travelling is to taste locally produced, fresh, fresh fruit: White Italian peaches, Kenyan mango, Chinese pears, Mexican oranges. It is pretty hard to beat fresh fruit, eaten as it is, with the juice dribbling down your chin.

This will be rather a short section if I just said "peel banana, eat banana!" The classic variation is to mix the fruit up into a fruit salad (if you want with some passion fruit and lemon juice sprinkled over the top). It's simple, and always tastes delicious.

The other thing you can try is adding something to the fruit. The simplest thing is to caramelise it. Do this by sprinkling the cooked fruit with sugar (it's best with dark brown sugar but you can use whatever is to hand) and then put some hot metal (maybe lift up the grate and use that, alternatively use a heated knife) onto it to caramelise the sugar. The next way is to give it a kick. Heat up some alcohol – not too hot though, as it evaporates at 80 degrees – pour it over your fruit. Carefully ignite the alcohol too if you fancy. Or give the fruit a glaze: pour honey and flaked nuts over the fresh or cooked fruit

Or you can make a sauce. A good thing to try is a 'butter'. This means you'll need some butter or margarine. Melt it and add things to give it flavour: say ginger, sugar and some alcohol. You could change the ginger for herbs or spices if you have them. Some of this butter can be put on the food just before you cook it, the rest can be dribbled over when its done.

Less buttery and a bit thicker are sauces that use milk as the base. This can be heated up gently and sugar (again, brown is best) can be added. Only use a little bit of milk as it will take quite a lot of sugar. The brown sugar will turn the milk into butterscotch. Don't let it boil though, pour it from the pot over your fruit.

More sugary is just to put some sugar into your pot and, over a gentle heat let it turn to liquid. When it become thick and syrupy add a big knob of butter and take it off the heat. The butter will melt as you stir it in. You can add alcohol or fruit juice too if you like. You can also put some citrus zest into the mixture.

BARBECUED FRUIT

You can put fruit straight onto the grate, or you can skewer it to make a kebab. Try everything.

For example, take a pineapple and cut it in half lengthways and take out the core. Cook it on the flesh side first, for a minute or so, then turn it over and cook it for another four or five minutes. Either eat it like that or put something else in the middle.

Very soft fruits can turn into mush so avoid this by, for example keep bananas in their skins and cook for 7 or 8 minutes turning occasionally. Don't be surprised when the skin goes brownish black, that's supposed to happen!

RICE PUDDING

Rice – white and not long grain , Water, Milk, Sugar to taste, Saffron (optional),
Cardamom (optional), Almonds (optional)

For the daddy and the mammy of all backpacking feasts, and if you can get all the optional ingredients, go for it, and make my ultimate Afghani rice pudding. First thing is to get the cardamom to release its flavour. Put a few pods in a little water and put on the heat. You will smell when they are ready, trust your senses. Put the almonds in a pot and boil them hard for about 10 or 15 minutes. Tip away the water, slip the almonds out of their skins and chop them thinly lengthways. To prepare the saffron, put a few strands or grains into a little water over some heat. Leave it on the heat only for a minute or two. Put the rice in a pot and cover it well with water, put it on the heat and let it cook until it is soft – softer than you would have it normally. Add the spices and stir. Add the sugar and almonds and then some milk (just enough to make the mixture turn creamy). There it is. If you're not making it Afghani style, try adding some nutmeg or cinnamon. You can also serve the rice pudding over fruit.

COMPOTE

Get your fruit, anything will work, peel, de-seed and de-core as necessary, cut into pieces and put in your pot. Sprinkle generously with sugar and cover with water. Bring to the boil, stir occasionally. It is ready when it has become a soft mush. Pineapple and orange work well together, as do banana and passion fruit, and mango and rum (but add the rum at the last minute otherwise it will evaporate). Adding nuts can give a nice change in texture.

FRIED FRUIT

Take your fruit, put a knob of butter or margarine in the pot and fry it. You can add spices to the butter if you want.

POACHED FRUIT

Fruit, Water, Anything to infuse in the water (optional)

Peel the fruit (I find this is only worth doing with firm things like apples and pears) leaving the stem on. Cut out the core from the base rub some lemon juice over the fruit to stop it discolouring. Immerse them in cold water (which you may have added something aromatic to) and bring this to the boil then let it simmer with a lid on for about 30 minutes or until the fruit is tender. Take it out carefully and slice it. To make it haute cuisine, only slice up to a point near the stem and then fan it out.

NOTES

1. TEAR ALONG THIS DOTTED LINE

5. INSERT THIS END
INTO THE CHARCOAL
STOVE (SIRIGI)

3. PLACE PILE OF ASH
IN GREY ZONE

4. ADD METHS OR
PARAFFIN TO ASH
PILE

2. FOLD UP ALONG
THIS DASHED LINE

6. LIGHT HERE

IF ALL ELSE FAILS,
USE THIS PAGE AS
AN EMERGENCY
FIRELIGHTER.

THE POPULAR
PREMIUM PALLIS
PAPER PYRO PRIMER

PATENT PENDING